Keeping *Unusual* Pets

FERRETS

June McNicholas

Heinemann Library
Chicago, Illinois

Customer Service 888-454-2279
Visit our website at www.heinemannlibrary.com

Designed by Celia Floyd
Originated by Dot Gradations Limited
Printed in China

07 06
10 9 8 7 6 5

Library of Congress Cataloging-in-Publication Data

McNicholas, June, 1956-
  Ferrets / June McNicholas.
      p. cm. -- (Keeping unusual pets)
Includes bibliographical references (p.   ).
  ISBN 1-40340-281-7
  1. Ferrets as pets--Juvenile literature. [1. Ferrets as pets. 2.
Pets.] I. Title. II. Series.
  SF459.F47 M36 2002
  636.9'76628--dc21

                        2002003162

Acknowledgments
The author and publishers are grateful to the following for permission to reproduce copyright material:
pp. 4 (top), 4 (bottom), 40 Corbis; pp. 5, 6, 7 (top), 8, 9, 10, 11, 12 (bottom), 13, 14 (top), 14 (bottom), 15 (top), 15 (bottom), 16 (left), 16 (right), 17 (top), 17 (bottom), 18, 19 (top), 19 (bottom), 20 (top), 20 (bottom), 21 (top), 21 (bottom), 22 (top), 22 (bottom), 23, 24 (top), 24 (bottom), 25 (top), 25 (bottom), 26, 27, 28, 29 (top), 29 (bottom), 30 (left), 30 (right), 31 (top), 31 (bottom), 32 (top), 32 (bottom), 33 (top), 33 (bottom), 35, 36, 37, 38, 39, 41, 42, 43 (top), 43 (bottom), 44 (left), 44 (right), 45 (top), 45 (bottom left), 45 (bottom right) Dave Bradford/Aylesbury Studios; p. 12 (top) Maria Joannou; p. 34 Tudor Photography.

Cover photograph reproduced with permission of Photodisc.

Every effort has been made to contact copyright holders of any material reproduced in this book. Any omissions will be rectified in subsequent printings if notice is given to the publisher.

Some words are shown in bold, **like this.** You can find out what they mean by looking in the glossary.

No animals were harmed during the process of taking photographs for this series.

Contents

What Is a Ferret?

Ferrets are not wild animals. Except for the very rare black-footed ferret that lives in the United States, there is no such thing as a wild ferret. Ferrets have been **domesticated** by humans for hundreds of years. They do not behave like wild animals and are not afraid of people.

Ferrets are **mammals.** That means they are **warm-blooded,** give birth to live babies, and feed their babies with milk. They belong to the **mustelid** family, which includes polecats, weasels, minks, otters, wolverines, and badgers.

The black-footed ferret is the only ferret that lives in the wild. It is now extremely rare and in danger of becoming **extinct.**

Strong smells

Mustelids have small scent glands all over their body, and full-grown male mustelids can have a strong smell. Mustelids also have special scent glands under their tail. These glands can give off a really bad smell if an animal is very frightened or hurt. However, the smell passes very quickly. If a pet ferret escapes or gets lost, it can give off a bad smell to keep dogs or foxes from attacking it. The bad smell can be a good thing!

Polecats are wild animals that are closely related to ferrets. The first ferrets were probably **bred** from polecats.

4

Working ferrets

Ferrets are excellent hunters and love chasing through tunnels. Drawings from the 11th century show women using ferrets to help them chase rabbits out of their burrows and into waiting nets. Many ferrets today are still used to hunt rabbits, but they are also very popular as pets.

Ferrets are used as working animals in many parts of the world. But they also make playful and intelligent pets.

Need to know

- Several areas of the U.S. have laws against keeping ferrets as pets. Check with your local **breeder,** pet store, or vet before bringing home your new pet.
- Most countries have laws protecting animals. It is your responsibility to make sure your ferret is healthy and well cared for. Always take your pet to the veterinarian if it is ill or injured.
- You are legally responsible for your ferret's care and its behavior. Think about **insuring** your ferret. You can find out about insurance for your pet through a ferret club or vet.

Ferret Facts

Ferrets are very playful and enjoy human company. They can be **house-trained** so they will not make a mess on your floor. They make very little noise and they usually do not chew wires or cables. But this does not mean they are trouble-free or boring!

Ferrets can be very active— they are usually either racing around or sound asleep! When they are awake, they like to explore everything. You need to keep them happy and occupied with lots of company, toys, and activities. Luckily, ferrets are not **nocturnal**, so they tend to be awake at the same time as you.

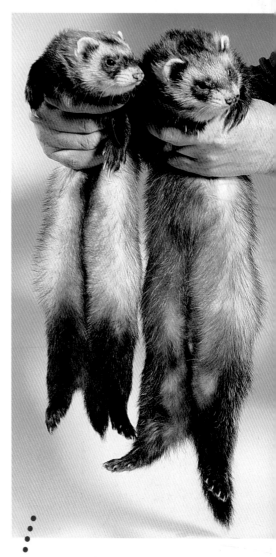

A hob (right) is bigger than a jill (left), but they both make excellent pets.

Hobs and jills

Male ferrets are called **hobs** and female ferrets are called **jills.** Hobs are usually larger than jills. They weigh around 3 to 5 pounds (1.5 to 2.2 kg) and are about 18 to 24 inches (45 to 60 cm) long. Jills weigh around 1 to 3 pounds (.5 to 1.5 kg) and are about 12 to 16 inches (30 to 40 cm) long. Both hobs and jills put on a lot of extra weight in the winter. They sometimes gain more than a quarter of their total summer body weight! But they soon lose it again.

Young ferrets are usually born in the spring and early summer. They are called **kits.** The average life span of a ferret is about seven years, although many live for up to ten years and some live even longer.

Different colors

Ferrets come in a variety of colors and their coats have a range of markings. Here are some of the main ferret colors and patterns:

- Sable ferrets have an all-brown body, though the color can range from light brown to dark red-brown. Sable ferrets can also have a white face with a black or brown "face mask."
- White ferrets range from pure white to a "blond" tint. Occasionally, white ferrets will have black spots, usually on the head.
- Pure **albino** ferrets do exist, but are extremely rare.
- Silvermitt ferrets have a white or yellow undercoat, with a "frosting" of gray, black, or brown fur on top.

The ferrets on the left are a sandy ferret and a silvermitt. But as you can see from the picture above, there are lots of colors to choose from!

Is a Ferret for You?

Ferrets can look cute and fun, but are they the right pet for you? And are you the right person to be a ferret owner? If you and your ferret do not suit one another, you may make each other very unhappy. So how do you decide?

As with any pet, there are good things and not-so-good things about owning a ferret. Here are some of the pluses and minuses of owning a ferret that you should think about.

Ferret good points

- Ferrets are intelligent and friendly.
- They are playful and entertaining.
- They can live for seven years or more.
- They can live indoors or outdoors.
- They are not **nocturnal,** so they are active when you are.
- They are naturally clean; they use only one corner of their housing as a toilet.
- They will play in the house with you.
- They can be taken for walks on a **harness.**

Many children enjoy having curious ferrets as pets.

8

Ferret not-so-good points

- Ferrets have a noticeable smell. This is usually not a problem in **neutered** animals, but some people find it unpleasant.
- Even neutered ferrets can give off a very bad smell if they are frightened or hurt.
- It can be expensive to set up your ferret's home.
- You will have to exercise and play with your ferret for at least two hours a day.
- Ferrets need to have their cage cleaned out, and be given food and water, at least once a day.
- A ferret can bite hard if it is frightened or hurt.
- Your ferret will need regular **vaccinations** and health checks, and it may also need to be treated for illnesses. Vet visits can be expensive.

Ferrets are not naturally destructive, but they are experts at "rearranging" things. If they can reach something, they may wreck it!

Yes or no?

So, can you handle the chores? Now is the time to be honest with yourself. If the answer is "no," then maybe you should think of a different pet that requires less care.

Can you make a promise to your future ferret to be responsible for its health and happiness? Will you look after it even when you are in a hurry or want to do something else? If the answer is "yes," you may have just made the decision to own a ferret!

Choosing Your Ferret

It is important to meet and handle as many ferrets as you can before you finally decide to be a ferret owner. You could try contacting local ferret clubs to find out where and when events are being held. Then you could go talk to ferret owners and meet their pets.

One ferret or two?

Ferrets like to have company, so it is usually best to have two **neutered** ferrets. Try to buy them together as **kits.** It is possible to introduce adult ferrets to each other, but this should be done gradually. You may need the advice of an experienced ferret owner to make sure your ferrets make friends with each other. If you can only keep one ferret, you will have to make sure that you give it all the time and company it needs.

Hob or jill?

Both **hobs** and **jills** make good pets, but both sexes should be neutered. This will stop the male ferrets from smelling so strongly. It will also mean that you can keep hobs and jills together. If your ferret is not already neutered when you buy it, you will need to take it to the vet for a simple operation. Neutered ferrets can live happily in same sex or mixed sex groups.

Take your time choosing a ferret. You and your pet will have to like each other and live together for many years!

Buying your ferret

You should buy your ferret from someone who has been recommended to you by another ferret owner, by a member of a ferret club, or by your vet. It is not a good idea to buy from pet stores unless they can tell you where the ferret came from. The shop owner should also be able to show you how well the ferret can be handled.

What to look for

It is best to buy a young ferret, but kits should be at least eight to ten weeks old before they leave their mother. Whether you are looking for a kit or an adult, there are a few basic things to look for:

- The ferret should be living in clean surroundings.
- It should have bright eyes, clean ears, and a soft, clean coat.
- It should be friendly and not frightened of you.
- It should be willing to be handled.

Top tip

Watch how the person looking after the ferrets picks them up. If the ferret keeper is confident, the ferrets are probably used to being handled.

This ferret has bright eyes and looks lively and alert. It would make a good pet.

What Do I Need?

The two most important pieces of equipment you will need for your ferret are a strong cage or **hutch,** and a secure play area.

The cage

Your ferret's cage will be its main home. Ferrets are active, so you must have a roomy cage. For one or two ferrets, the cage should be at least 50 inches (120 cm) wide, 35 inches (90 cm) deep, and 25 inches (60 cm) high, or even bigger if possible.

Ferrets are strong animals, so most rabbit hutches will need to be fitted with extra strong wire and door latches to make them ferret-proof. The cage will also need a separate sleeping area for when the ferrets need privacy and quiet.

Although some people use wooden cages, metal cages like the one on the right are far more common.

Top tips

- Avoid cages with wire-mesh floors because they are uncomfortable for a ferret's soft feet.
- A two-story cage will give lots of space and height for an upstairs bedroom, a ramp, and downstairs feeding, play, and toilet areas.

Indoors or out?

Ferrets can live indoors or outdoors. If your ferret is going to live indoors, put its cage in a place where it will not be in cold drafts. Ferrets do not like extreme heat, so do not put the cage close to a radiator. It is also important to make sure that the cage is not in a place where other animals can bother or frighten your ferret.

If you choose to keep your ferret outside, the cage must be protected from wind, rain, and bad weather. A weatherproof cover is essential to drape over the hutch. You also need to protect the hutch from hot sun. Ferrets can die from **heatstroke,** so make sure that your ferret has plenty of shade in hot weather. Remember that an outdoor ferret also needs to be safe from wild animals like raccoons, as well as neighboring cats and dogs.

Cage furnishings

Before you bring your ferret home, make sure you have everything it will need to settle into its new cage.

A cozy bed

The sleeping area should have a box to act as a bed, with blankets or shredded paper to burrow into. Do not use material with loose fibers that can catch on your ferret's claws. In addition to blankets or shredded paper, you can also add some straw or hay. Straw is good in summer, and hay makes cozy winter bedding. Only buy hay and straw from good pet shops to be sure there are no fleas or **ticks** in it.

You can use a crate with some old blankets and towels to make a cozy bed for your ferret.

Ferret toys

Your ferret will appreciate having toys. Try some of these:
- tubes wide enough to run through
- a hay net or a box of straw or shredded paper
- a hammock to bounce in or sleep in
- a ball on a rope, hung from the cage ceiling
- a cat ball with a bell in it.

Food and water bowls

You will need two bowls—one for food and another for water. They should be heavy enough so your ferret cannot turn them upside down! Or you can buy bowls that clip onto the wires of the cage. Most ferrets think their water bowl is for swimming and love splashing the water around! If you don't mind the puddles, let your ferrets enjoy playing with their water. But make sure they always have enough to drink by clipping a water bottle to the wire of their cage.

Ferrets love to play with bowls and tubs, so make sure that your pet's food bowl is too heavy for it to overturn.

Bathroom corner

Ferrets usually use only one corner of their cage as a toilet. This is most often the corner furthest away from their bed. Your ferret will decide which corner it wants—and you won't be able to change its mind! Line this corner with newspaper or sawdust and clean it out at least once a day.

Some ferrets learn to use cat litter boxes, but your ferret might just kick the box out of the way. You could try using cat litter in the litter corner, but most ferrets will prefer to just throw it around.

Your ferret will have hours of fun bouncing around in a hammock. You can make your own hammock from an old cushion cover or a pillowcase.

15

Exercise areas

Your ferret will need regular daily playtimes out of its cage, either in the house with you, or in an outdoor run. The advantage of letting your ferret play indoors is that it will become part of the family and everyone can enjoy it. The disadvantage is that you will need to "ferret-proof" your home!

A ferret-proof home

If you let your ferret run around inside, make sure it cannot climb into fireplaces or get trapped behind chairs or stuck inside cabinets. Always let other members of the family know that your ferret is out of its cage. You do not want them stepping on your pet or leaving doors open for it to escape.

Never leave your ferret alone because you can never tell what it will get into! Watch out for your houseplants and move anything breakable out of the way. Some ferrets scratch at carpets, especially in front of doors. A rug, sheet of newspaper, or a piece of plastic carpet protector can prevent any damage.

Some strong **hobs** learn how to open cabinets and refrigerators.

Once your refrigerator is opened, it will soon be emptied!

Ferrets are not interested in the plants and flowers—they just want to scatter the soil as far as possible!

An outdoor run

A run with an area measuring six feet by three feet (two meters by one meter) will be large enough for a couple of ferrets. Strong mesh on a wooden frame will make a good run. The floor will need to be meshed too, to stop ferrets from digging tunnels or squeezing underneath the frame. Cover the floor with soil, peat, sawdust, or something similar so that the mesh does not hurt the ferrets' feet. Ferrets can climb well, so fix a strong top or lid onto the run that can be locked securely.

Put a bedding box inside the run so your ferrets can take a nap, and do not forget to provide food and water. Position the run in a sheltered area, protected from the weather. You can use a **tarp** to provide extra cover.

The advantage of an outdoor play area is that ferrets can be left on their own. But your pet will still need human company and you have to make time every day to handle your ferret and play with it.

Caring for Your Ferret

Ferrets are **carnivorous** animals, which means they eat meat. But fresh meat is not enough on its own. The best food to give your pet is one of the specially made dried foods for ferrets. These foods contain all the **protein** and **vitamins** your ferret needs to stay healthy, and they are more **hygienic** than raw meat. Never feed your ferret bread and milk. Many ferrets get upset stomachs if they drink milk.

This picture shows the difference between ferret food (top) and cat food (bottom). Cat food and dog food pieces are larger than ferret food pieces and could get stuck in your pet's throat. They also may not contain enough protein for ferrets.

Top Tips

- There are several good ferret foods on the market. Whichever you choose, always follow the feeding instructions on the label.
- Unless your ferret is very greedy, you can leave a bowl of dried food in its cage all the time so it can help itself.
- Many ferrets like to eat small amounts, rather than a large meal all at once.

18

Make sure your ferret has fresh water every day. You can use a heavy bowl or a bottle that clips onto the side of the cage.

Not too much

Do not overfeed your ferret! Most ferrets are good at eating the right amount and do not become overweight. But some can be greedy, so you need to keep an eye on them. Remember that most ferrets will put on a lot of weight in the winter, but if your pet gets very fat, it may be eating too much. If your ferret has a fat stomach but it is not eating a lot, take it to see a veterinarian. Sometimes this can be a sign of illness.

Treats

Some ferrets love treats, but you need to be careful not to feed them things that are bad for them. It is best to buy tasty treats and **vitamin supplements** that are specially made for ferrets. Candy and chocolates are particularly bad for ferrets. They can make a ferret very fat and give it bad teeth. Suitable "healthy" treats are a little boiled or scrambled egg, and very small amounts of white fish.

Most ferrets love ice cream. It is not really good for them, but you can give your pet a tiny amount as a very special treat.

Keeping clean

Your ferret's bathroom corner should be cleaned at least once a day. Once a week you should clean all the surfaces in your ferret's cage with a cloth soaked in a mild disinfectant. Food and water bowls should be washed daily, and check your pet's bedding to make sure it is clean and dry. Bedding and hammocks should be changed and washed every week.

Grooming

Ferrets **groom** their own fur, but twice a year they lose a large amount of their old coat and grow new fur—this is called **molting**.

Hold your ferret firmly while you shampoo its fur.

Bath time

Ferrets rarely need bathing. If your ferret gets dirty, or if you are taking it to a show, you can wash it with a special ferret shampoo.

- Do not cover the ferret in water—just dip it in lukewarm water and then hold it above the water.
- Gently shampoo your ferret's coat, avoiding its face and eyes.
- Dip it again in the water, to rinse it.
- Dry it with a clean towel and then stand back while it runs around the room to get really dry!
- Do not let your ferret get cold, and make sure it is absolutely dry before going outside.

After you have finished shampooing your ferret, rinse it thoroughly and then dry it.

Top tip

It can be easier to use a dry shampoo on your ferret than to wash it in water. Dry shampoo is a powder that is brushed into the ferret's coat and then brushed out again. Dry shampooing is a good idea when the weather is very cold, or for ferrets that hate baths!

Nail care

Ferrets' nails grow quite quickly, so you will need to cut them regularly. Place your ferret's paw flat on the palm of your hand. If its nails dig into your hand, they need cutting. Having its nails cut does not hurt the ferret, but most ferrets do not like it much. It is a good idea to get another person to hold the ferret while you do the trimming.

Most ferrets have pale nails, so it is easy to see the red vein in each claw. Do not clip too close to this vein as it will pinch and hurt the ferret or even make it bleed. Use ordinary nail clippers and be careful not to cut the vein.

It can help to give your ferret a treat while its nails are being trimmed. There are lots of tasty liquid **vitamin** treats that will keep your pet occupied.

21

Checking your ferret

It is important to check your ferret regularly to make sure it is fit and healthy.

- Check your ferret all over each day for any lumps, bumps, or sore spots.
- Check that your ferret's teeth are clean and its gums are a healthy pink.
- Check your pet's nails to see that they are not broken or too long.
- Check your ferret's bathroom corner for any unusual **feces.**
- Check for fleas and **ticks,** especially if your ferret goes out for walks in fields or is in contact with cats, dogs, or other animals.
- Check that your pet's ears are clean. A weekly wipe with a tissue is usually all that is needed. Never poke inside a ferret's ears with cotton swabs.

If you find anything unusual, talk to an adult or a veterinarian about your concerns.

These are normal ferret feces. If your ferret's feces look abnormal, you should tell an adult and contact a veterinarian.

You can buy special ear-cleaning tissues from pet stores to wipe inside your pet's ears. Do it very gently and never poke anything inside an animal's ears.

Vacation care

Ferrets need daily care. If you are away for a short period, such as a couple of days, it is best to ask a friend or neighbor to visit your ferret every day to clean out its cage and give it food, water, and exercise. Choose someone who knows and likes your ferret and who you can trust to look after your pet for you. Make sure you leave clear instructions about exercise times, when to feed your pet, and how much food to give. Leave your vet's phone number behind in case there is an emergency.

If you will be away for a longer period of time, you will need to find someone who will **board** your ferret. Ferret clubs and vets often have details of people willing to board ferrets. Make all your arrangements well in advance. Some boarders may require that your ferret has up-to-date **vaccinations.**

Going on vacation

Some people take their ferret on vacation with them. Your ferret will need a secure traveling box and a suitable cage to live in while it is on vacation. If you take your pet for a walk, be sure it has your vacation address and telephone number on its collar or **harness,** in case it gets lost.

You can take your ferret on trips in a pet carrier like this one. Remember to put some food, a water bottle, and a blanket in the carrier if you are traveling more than a few miles.

Making Friends

Do not expect instant friendship from your ferret. It takes time to get to know each other. Your pet will need to settle into its cage for a day or two before you start to handle it.

Easy does it

Start by talking to your ferret while it is in its cage so that it gets used to your voice. Do not try to handle it if it is hungry or tired. Hungry ferrets mistake fingers for food and tired ferrets may be grumpy. Offer your pet some food and gently stroke its back while it eats.

Try stroking your ferret gently while it is busy eating. Avoid making sudden movements or noises that might startle it.

Picking up your ferret

When you are sure your ferret is happy being touched, pick it up with one hand behind its front legs and the other hand supporting its bottom. If it relaxes, you can support its bottom against your body and stroke it with your free hand. With time, you will be able to hold your pet draped over your arm or lying in your arms on its back like a baby! However, do not rush things; you both need time to learn to trust each other.

Holding your ferret securely will help you to build a trusting relationship with your pet.

Before very long, your ferret will relax and become very friendly!

Special care

If you get an adult ferret from a rescue shelter, it may have had unkind owners in the past. You will have to teach it to trust people again. This requires extra time and patience. It is very worthwhile in the end, so don't give up.

Top tip

Do not put your ferret near your face until it is completely happy being picked up. Some ferrets grab noses and chins!

Your ferret can become great friends with your cat or dog, but let them get used to each other slowly.

Meeting other pets

Ferrets can get along well with cats and dogs. But the first time you introduce them, make sure your ferret is safely in its cage. This is a safe way to see how they will react to each other. Ferrets are natural hunters of rabbits and small animals, so you should never let them near pet rabbits, guinea pigs, hamsters, rats, gerbils, or other small animals or birds.

Nip or bite?

There is a difference between a ferret nip and a bite. Ferrets use their teeth in play and they do not always know that these play nips can hurt you. **Kits** may nip a lot because they are overexcitable—they have just not grown up enough to be very careful.

Do not punish a ferret of any age for playing with you. Distract your pet by offering it an interesting toy, such as something to chase or jump on. Then pick up your ferret and stroke it gently and soothingly until it calms down. A good tip is to feed your ferret before you handle it. That way it will not be hungry enough to think that your hand is food and it will be too full to get too excited.

Safety first

If your ferret nips or bites you and draws blood, tell an adult. They might decide to consult a doctor if the bite is bad. You should wash the bite with soap and water.

Your ferret may sometimes get overexcited and give you a small nip. These play nips do not usually hurt.

Painful bites

A real bite is painful. The ferret may hang onto your hand and really sink its teeth in. But why does it do this? Usually this happens because your ferret is frightened or hurt, or because it is not ready to trust people yet. Do not be too upset. Just start again by making friends slowly with your ferret. It is very rare for a ferret to remain bad tempered if it is treated kindly. However, if you need any help, call a ferret club, pet society, or vet for advice. They have lots of experience in helping new owners.

Use a toy to distract your ferret if it is nipping a lot. Then stroke it gently until it calms down.

Hanging on

Occasionally, a ferret might hold your finger firmly without biting, but still show no signs of wanting to let go! It probably wants to take you somewhere. Let it lead you wherever it wants. It will let go of your finger when it gets bored, although it may try stuffing you into its play tube or dragging you under the sofa first!

Top tip

Always be patient with your ferret. It is better to take things very slowly and get it right than to rush it. If you make a mistake, it will upset both you and your ferret, and it will take time to put things right again.

27

Fun and Games

Ferrets are fun-loving creatures and need lots of playtime and toys. It will be up to you to stop your ferret from getting fat, lazy, or bored.

How ferrets play

Ferrets play by bouncing, pouncing, and rolling around on the floor. They do a lot of sideways dancing, often with their mouths open, and while they dance they make little hissing or chuckling noises. Ferrets will pretend to attack you or anything that moves. It sometimes looks as if they are chasing something that only they can see!

A friend for your ferret?

Play is very important to ferrets, so think about how to keep your pet occupied. The best thing for a ferret to play with is another ferret, so consider keeping two ferrets, if possible. Ferrets are sociable animals and like the company of other ferrets. Two ferrets can be twice as much fun for their owner.

When ferrets play, they can look like they have gone crazy! Some people call the way they play "the weasel war-dance."

28

One ferret

If you can only keep one ferret, you will have to make sure that you give your pet all the time and company it needs. Otherwise, it could get lonely. You could think about contacting a rescue shelter. Shelters often have ferrets that have always lived on their own and need to be kept as a single pet.

Ferrets love racing through tubes. You could set up a complete obstacle course for your pet, with tubes to chase through and blocks to climb over.

Playtime

Whether you have one ferret or two, you will still need to give your pet exercise and playtime.

- Make sure you have a secure area where your ferret can play safely.
- Spend some time every day having fun with your ferret.
- You could try ferret racing games with tubes, bends, and tunnels. Some ferret clubs have special races, although they are held more for fun than for serious competition.

Toys for your ferret

There are lots of ferret toys in pet shops, but you can make your own much more cheaply. This means you can give your pet a change of toys more often. Ferrets can get bored if they play with the same toys all the time!

Ferrets love playing with crinkly bags. But make a hole in plastic bags so your pet does not get stuck and suffocate.

Ferret favorites

- Tubes and tunnels: These are real favorites. You can use plastic piping or tubes that have been used for carpet rolls. But first make sure that they are wide enough!
- Large crinkly paper bags: Ferrets love the noise they make.
- Hammocks: Make a hammock from a cushion cover, a pillowcase, or something similar. Do not use anything with loose threads that a ferret's nails can get caught in. Tie or hook each corner of the hammock to the top of the ferret cage or play area. Within minutes, your ferret will be using it like a trampoline.

Water play

Some ferrets love to splash in water, but others hate it. Use a wide, shallow dish that a ferret can jump in and out of. Some ferrets will "snorkel" by putting their noses underwater and blowing bubbles. Others try to "dig" at the water, and some climb in completely. Only allow ferrets to play in water during warm weather, and always dry them thoroughly before putting them back in their cage.

Digging and burrowing

Ferrets will enjoy burrowing into a good-sized bowl of dry soil or soil substitute. This can get messy, so be prepared to clean it up!

Other toys

Your ferret will enjoy other toys, such as cat balls, tassels hung from the cage roof, or just bundles of shredded paper. Boxes with ferret-sized holes cut into them are also great fun.

Try dangling a ball on a string just above your ferret. Soon it will be leaping and twisting to grab at the ball.

Your ferret will spend hours unwrapping packages, especially if there is a lot of noisy paper to play with!

Safety first

Never give your ferret toys made from soft rubber or sponge. It might take bites out of these, and pieces could get stuck in its throat or stomach. Also avoid soft wool materials that can catch on its claws.

Walking your ferret

Some ferrets love walks. Others just refuse to cooperate, although they enjoy being carried around. It is unkind to force an unwilling ferret to go for walks.

You will need a **harness** and a leash. Choose a brightly colored harness. If your ferret does get lost, someone should notice the harness and realize that they have found a lost pet. Attach a small tag to the harness with your telephone number on it.

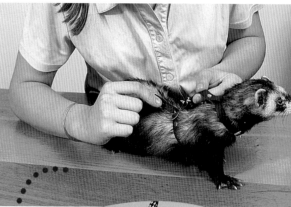

Buy a harness with two straps. Fit one strap over the head, and fasten the second strap behind the front legs. Then attach the leash securely.

Top tips

- Most dogs will never have seen a ferret and may want to chase it or snap at it. If you see a dog coming, pick your ferret up and hold it until the dog passes by.
- Do not let your ferret go down holes or in places where you cannot safely reach it.
- Do not walk your ferret on hot, sunny days or if it is very cold or wet. A short playtime in snow is a real treat, but do not let your ferret get too cold.

Where should we go?

A ferret will expect you to go wherever it wants! Just when you think you are going in a straight line, your ferret may dive into the bushes or show that it wants to be picked up.

After a walk, always check your ferret for pieces of twig or grass that may get matted into its coat. Check for fleas or **ticks** if you have been walking in areas where there are wild animals.

Ferrets tend to walk better on a path or a track. Open fields seem to confuse them. This may be because they have very poor eyesight. Ferrets will often recognize a familiar path and pull ahead on their leash, almost running.

Make sure your ferret is dry and comfortable after its walk, and give it a snack and a drink. Then settle it down in its cage for a well-earned rest. You will probably need one too.

Staying Healthy

Besides you, the most important person in your ferret's life is its vet. You may already know a vet in your area, or other ferret owners may have recommended one to you.

There are two very important things you need to do to keep your ferret healthy. You should get it **vaccinated** once a year, and you should have it **neutered.** You will need to visit your vet to get these things done. Your vet will talk to you and your parents about why these procedures are necessary.

Protect your pet!

Your ferret will need a yearly vaccination for **canine distemper.** This is done by your vet. The injection is vital if your ferret is in contact with dogs or visits places where dogs walk. It is a simple injection that will protect your ferret from a disease that could kill it.

Neutering

Breeding ferrets is not recommended. A **jill** may give birth to as many as a dozen **kits,** and it can be difficult to find good homes for all of them. It is much better for you and your ferret if you have it neutered.

Neutering is a surgical operation to prevent ferrets from breeding. Besides preventing unwanted babies, neutering has other advantages. **Hobs** become more friendly and playful, and lose their strong smell. Jills should also be neutered because this protects them from some illnesses. Ferrets cope with the operation very well and recover quickly after resting for a few days.

This jill has just been neutered. You can see where she was shaved for her operation.

35

Some Health Problems

Although it is really easy to take care of ferrets, sometimes they get ill, just like you do. Here are some of the common problems you might experience with your ferret.

Stomach problems

Each time you clean out your ferret's bathroom corner, check its **feces** to see if they look normal. If the feces are normal colored but rather runny, then your ferret may have simple diarrhea. This may be caused by a sudden change in food, too much milk, ice cream, raw eggs, or other treats. If this seems a likely cause and your ferret is healthy in other ways, give it a very plain diet for a day or so, with no treats or extras. This will often give its stomach a rest and take care of the problem.

For some problems, your ferret may need to take some medicine. One of the easiest ways to give it medicine is by using a dropper.

If your ferret's feces are more abnormal, such as greenish colored, jelly-like, very smelly, or if they have blood in them, your ferret may have an infection. You will need to see a vet quickly. Dark, thread-like feces sometimes mean the ferret has eaten something that has blocked its intestines. Again, you should get to your veterinarian quickly.

Toothache

Ferrets often chip their teeth when they are playing. A chipped tooth will discolor and turn gray over time. This is not a problem unless it causes pain. A ferret with a toothache may paw at its mouth and be obviously in pain when it eats. It may also not eat its food, drool, dribble, and look uncomfortable. Your ferret may need to have a tooth taken out. Your vet will put your ferret to sleep for a short while and then remove the painful tooth.

Bad breath

Bad breath is usually caused by bad teeth or infected gums. It is not common in younger ferrets that have been fed a proper diet, but older ferrets sometimes develop these problems.

Check your ferret's mouth at least once a week. Red and sore-looking gums mean infection, and dirty teeth may need to be cleaned by a vet.

Dirty ears

A little yellowish-brown wax in your ferret's ears is normal. Dark brown, gritty-looking wax may mean a ferret has **ear mites.** These are tiny creatures that can cause pain and discomfort to your ferret. Ear mites can be easily treated with ear drops from your vet. But left untreated, they may travel deep into your ferret's ear, causing it to lose its sense of balance. If your ferret has itchy ears, or holds its head tilted to one side, it needs urgent treatment. Prevention is the best cure, and weekly ear checks will catch any mite problem early.

Colds

You are very unlikely to catch anything from your ferret, but your pet might catch a cold from you! Ferrets often catch human colds and flu, and **kits** or older ferrets may even die. A ferret with a cold will have similar symptoms to you—a cough, sneezing, runny eyes and nose, and a temperature. It will need a visit to the vet and some gentle nursing.

If you have a cold, handle your ferret as little as possible or get someone else to care for your pet until you are better.

Wounds, bites, and stings

Ferrets can get themselves into trouble and get hurt. They may also be stung by a wasp or a bee if one gets into their cage. Usually all you need to do is clean the area with a mild **antibiotic.** Make sure you remove any stinger or object still stuck in the wound. You must watch any wounds, bites, or stings to make sure an **abscess** does not form. This is a swelling that contains pus, and it will need to be cleaned by your vet.

Hair loss

Heavy hair loss is common when ferrets **molt.** They sometimes end up with bald tails!

- Hair loss usually only lasts for a few weeks, and it is nothing to worry about, if the ferret is otherwise fit and healthy.
- If your ferret becomes bald elsewhere, especially on the back and sides of its body, it might be something more serious. You should take it to a vet.

If your ferret cuts itself, clean the wound with a mild soap. A soothing ointment can help, too.

39

Parasites

Sometimes your ferret may have **internal parasites,** such as worms, living inside its intestines. Ferrets can get parasites by eating raw meat or dead animals. Even if you do not feed these things to your ferret, it may still pick something up when it is out on a walk.

External parasites, such as fleas and **ticks,** live on the ferret's skin. They are most commonly picked up from cows, sheep, or other animals. You can protect your ferret from parasites by regular **worming** and flea and tick treatments. Your vet or a ferret club will be happy to give you advice on this.

This is a magnified photograph of a tick. Ticks cling onto your ferret's skin and suck its blood. Your vet can give you something to help get rid of them.

Heatstroke

Ferrets do not pant or sweat, so they get hot very quickly. This can be dangerous. A ferret can collapse from **heatstroke** in temperatures around 80°F (27°C). A sunny part of the yard can quite easily reach this temperature. Help your ferret stay cool by providing lots of shade at all times of the day, a water bowl to splash in, and a damp towel to rub itself on. If your ferret is affected by the heat, roll it up in some cool, damp cloths and take it to a veterinarian.

Lumps

Ferrets can get lumps and bumps just about anywhere on their body, although the stomach and neck are common places. Vets may be able to treat them. They may be **abscesses** and can be drained and cleaned. Or they may be fatty lumps that are **benign.** In some cases a lump may be **cancerous** and it will need to be removed, if possible.

If you find a lump on your ferret, it is best to let a vet check it out.

Danger signs

If you see any of the following signs, you should tell an adult and contact a vet immediately:

- If there is blood in your ferret's **feces,** or you see blood coming from your ferret's mouth, ears, nose, or behind.
- If your ferret stops eating for a long time or starts to vomit.
- If your ferret suddenly collapses.
- If you suspect that your pet has a broken bone after a fall, or if your ferret has been crushed.
- If your ferret seems to be in pain when it goes to the bathroom.
- If your ferret's stomach suddenly becomes much bigger.
- If your ferret has a high temperature.
- If your ferret has an open wound or an abscess.

Saying Goodbye

Most ferrets only live for seven or eight years, so no matter how well you care for your pet, one day it will die. Sometimes a ferret will die peacefully and unexpectedly at home. This will come as a shock for you, but do not blame yourself. There is probably nothing that you could have done to keep it alive, and you will know that it didn't die in pain.

When ferrets get old, they become less energetic and spend more time resting.

A peaceful end

As a caring owner, the hardest responsibility of all is knowing when to let your pet be put to sleep to save it from suffering. Your ferret may be very old and in pain. Or it may have a serious illness that cannot be cured. Your vet will give it a small injection. This does not hurt—it just makes your pet sleepy. Before you can count to ten, your ferret will be asleep for the last time.

42

Feeling upset

However it happens, you will feel upset when a pet dies, especially if your ferret has been a friend for many years. It is perfectly normal for people–adults as well as children–to cry when a pet dies, or when they think of a dead pet. Eventually, the pain will go away and you will be left with the happy memories.

Sometimes it helps to have a special burial place for your pet.

Looking after your pet will have taught you a lot about ferrets. Maybe you will be able to give a home to another ferret that needs love and care.

Keeping a Record

It is fun to keep a record of your ferret, just like a family photo album. You can look back at it and remind yourself of what you did together as you and your ferret grew up.

Maybe you could start with a picture and the story of the first day your ferret came to live with you. How big was it? How did it change over the first year you had it? Did it look different in the summer and the winter?

Important dates

Keep a diary of important dates for your pet's health, such as its **vaccination** and **worming** dates. It is also good to record how your ferret's weight changes so that you can tell if it has put on or lost more weight than it did the previous year. When you take your ferret to the vet, take your scrapbook with you. It could be very useful.

You could make notes on the shows you went to with your ferret—and the prizes it won!

Top tip

Collect magazine articles on ferrets, cut them out, and keep them in your scrapbook.

Notes and pictures

You can keep a record of all sorts of things. When was the first day your ferret sat on your shoulders? Or went for a walk? Or met some visiting relatives? You could also take pictures of your pet playing with its favorite toys, and with other members of the family.

Choose a big scrapbook to fill—you and your ferret will enjoy many happy years together.

You will have lots of fun choosing pictures to go in your scrapbook.

Sharing the fun

You might like to take your ferret scrapbook to school and show it to your science teacher and your friends. You may find there are other people who keep ferrets too.

Glossary

abscess   soft lump full of pus, often caused by a bite or sting
albino   animal or person with very light or white skin, fur, or hair
antibiotic   medicine that fights infection
benign   not dangerous
board   look after an animal while its owner is away
breed   mate and then give birth to young
breeder   someone who keeps animals and encourages them to mate and produce young
cancerous   caused by cancer. Cancer is a disease that destroys the bdy's healthy cells.
canine distemper   serious disease, like the flu, that can kill dogs, ferrets, and some other animals
carnivorous   mainly meat-eating
domesticate   tame an animal so that it can live with humans
ear mite   small, spider-like creature that burrows into some animals' ears
external parasite   small creature, such as a tick, that lives on the body or in the fur of another animal
extinct   completely wiped out
feces   solid waste matter passed out of the body
groom   clean an animal's coat. Animals often groom themselves.
harness   set of straps that fit around an animal's body so you can take it for walks
heatstroke   illness caused by being too hot
hob   male ferret
house-train   train an animal to use a litter box or special toilet area

hutch   type of cage for a small animal
hygienic   clean and free from germs
insure   pay money to a company so that they will pay for the cost if you have an accident or a problem
internal parasite   small creature, such as a worm, that lives inside the body of another animal
jill   female ferret
kit   young ferret
mammal   animal with fur or hair on its body that feeds its babies with milk
molt   lose hair at particular times of the year, usually spring or summer
mustelid   member of the weasel family, such as a polecat or a ferret, that has special scent glands that produce a strong smell
neuter   to perform an operation that stops ferrets from having babies
nocturnal   active at night
parasite   small creature, such as a tick or worm, that lives on or in another animal's body
protein   important part of an animal's diet that helps it to grow and stay healthy
tarp   thick, waterproof cloth
tick   small creature that lives in the fur or on the skin of another animal
vaccinate   give an injection that protects against a disease
vitamin supplement   medicine or pills that provide extra vitamins
vitamin   important substance found in food that helps people and animals to stay healthy
warm-blooded   able to create body heat
worming   treating an animal in order to get rid of internal parasites, such as worms

Further Reading

Baglio, Ben. *Ferret Fun.* New York: Scholastic, Incorporated, 2000.

Bucsis, Gerry and Barbara Somerville. *The Ferret Handbook.* Hauppauge, N.Y.: Barron's Educational Series, Incorporated, 2001.

Crompton, Sheila. *All About Your Ferret.* Hauppauge, N.Y.: Barron's Educational Series, Incorporated, 1999.

Gelman, Amy. *My Pet Ferrets.* Minneapolis: Lerner Publishing Group, 2000.

Horton-Bussey, Claire, et. al. *101 Facts about Ferrets.* Milwaukee: Gareth Stevens Incorporated, 2002.

Paul, Christian. *Ferret Mania: Fantastic Facts and Furry Photos.* Mahwah, N.J.: Troll Communications L.L.C., 2002.

Shefferman, Mary R. and Eric. *Ferret Litter Box Training Manual: The Comprehensive Guide to Litter Box Training Your Pet.* Smithtown, N.Y.: Crunchy Concepts, Incorporated, 2001.

Useful Addresses

The American Ferret Association
626-C Admiral Dr. PMB 255
Annapolis, MD 21401
Tel: 1-888-FERRET-1
http://www.ferret.org/

National Alternative Pet Association
P.O. Box 369
Burnet, TX 78611
http://www.altpet.net/

Disclaimer
All Internet addresses (URLs) given in this book were valid at the time of going to press. However, due to the dynamic nature of the Internet, some addresses may have changed, or sites may have ceased to exist since publication. While the author and publisher regret any inconvenience this may cause readers, no responsibility for any such changes can be accepted by either the author or the publisher.

Index